TODO REVOLUCIONA

THANK you
FOR WELCOMING
ME HOME.

Angelica Mercado

Harsan Publishing

www.angelicamercado.com
@amercadowrites

"I will have my serpent's tongue,
My woman's voice,
My sexual voice,
My poet's voice.
I will overcome the tradition of silence."

-*Gloria E. Anzaldúa*

To fight for identity- to give value to the space in which you exist means power, and finding and fighting for that space is the ultimate war. In Todo Revoluciona, I tackle the tough issues in an attempt to embrace that divide. Therefore, my work demonstrates the constant state of confusion in which I stumble, fall, stand, fight and ultimately live in. With themes of loss, trauma, longing, healing, and overall finding a sense of belonging in this space I call home.

The day I chose the way out, I learned the way in.

-Rebirth

Tongues

My Pa lost his tongue
somewhere between El Rio Grande
y el Desierto de Sonora
while chasing the American Dream.
He did not notice its absence
until he opened his mouth
and what came out
was more white noise than melody.
The tongue- now shrunken and dried,
sits in the sand like a raisin.
The day he gave his naturalizing oath,
he was told to offer his heart as sacrifice
the temple- the country that replaced his tongue.

He now speaks with a recycled organ,
stressing syllables foreign to him,
foreign like him.

I tell him "Pa,
you lost your tongue
but there is nothing
in this world that can
be replaced,
only imitated.
Habla el Español
que tu sabes,
conduct melodies
in your own chest,
revive the heart,
the drum of life—
it is still yours."

Me, I am different,
my supple tongue
speaks for two.
Los dioses Aztecas
blessed me with a forked tongue,
like a double-headed serpent.

It rises,
each defending
her
territory,
her language,
her voz.

A ~~HOME~~
A HOUSE

A HOUSE DIVIDED TWO FLOORS
TWO OF EVERYTHING
TWO PARENTS
BUT NEVER WHOLE
TWO BODIES
TWO LANGUAGES

Ni de aquí, ni de allá,
Entonces de dónde?
De dónde?
De dónde?

Freedom is a Fleeting Thing
for Claudia Patricia Gomez Gonzalez,
murdered by U.S. border patrol on May 23rd, 2018

It is hard to imagine,
your face half dirt, half blood,
pressed against U.S. soil,
the only way this land will claim our kind.

"This is what happens you see?"
The agent reminds the three survivors,
as he places handcuffs on their brown,
sun-scorched skin.
A misdemeanor turned murder,
when he refused to acknowledge
that your eyes
held a story
many will never get to hear.

Two weeks ago, you promised mamita
a better life back home,
once you reached Virginia and your lover.
On the television screen,
your mother begs for your body
to be returned
'where it belongs.'

Princesita,
the world mourned you.

Still does.
We all have moments of silence,
when rage consumes us.
I often wonder if our voices still have sound.

Some days,
when silence fills the air,
I think about the children in cages,
their cries asking for any sign of familiarity,
from two lands who cannot raise them to take flight.
One they fled from,
and the other only knows how to spit them back.

Did you feel what freedom feels like,
before your eyes turned safety white?
Are you finally at peace?
I know San Juan Ostuncalco will always think of you,
Maya Nam hero.

This is what happens you see?
When it becomes too easy to
confuse human with animal,
pointing aim at life,
at anything that dares to interfere
with Manifest Destiny.

Claudia's dream did not belong in this America,
only in fictitious history textbooks,
making white man the hero
of every scenario,
disguising violence with promises of 'greatness.'
Lady Liberty has turned her back,
using the pretext of fear to close the golden gate.

This is no New Colossus.

In America, migrant dreams are flightless birds.
In America, you, the migrant
cannot dream, lest you are dead.

This is what happens, you see?
When the world becomes devoid of empathy,
filling in blanks with new names of the murdered,
of the lost,
of the forgotten.

To the ones in power: we demand action.
Words mean nothing
when Claudia cannot read, cannot see, cannot live.
When motherless children have dreams
of light-up sneakers
and survival.
Ejected from courtrooms
for their profane silence,
when their mouths have yet to hatch
the word *mamá*.

This is what happens, you see?
When borders become militarized weapons,
and bodies become numbers.
Claudia was only 19 years old.

Some nights,
I think I've made it.
In the moonlight,
my skin is iridescent.
Its pearly whiteness
teases me with privilege.

I shake it off.
Remember Claudia,
Remember the children.

Where are the children?

Nadie debe morir
Tratando de vivir.

Nadie debe morir
Tratando de vivir.

Nadie debe morir
Tratando de vivir.

Nadie debe morir
Tratando de vivir.

Nadie debe morir
Tratando de vivir.

Nadie debe morir
Tratando de vivir.

Nadie debe morir
Tratando de vivir.

Nadie debe morir
Tratando de vivir.

WE HAD TO LEAVE HER
THERE IN THE DESERT
SHE COULD NOT WALK/

SHE STARTED TO SWALLOW
SAND THINKING IT WAS
WATER/

THE TEARGAS KILLED THE
BABY AT THE BORDER/

I CANNOT SLEEP/
THE GIRL DID NOT GET
WATER SHE
WAS 7 YEARS
OLD.

A greedy homeland,
hungry for more,
yet its people,
centuries spent suffering
at the sharpening of its knife.

-when can you be called home again?

On Being Woman (in ten parts)

I

The day I lost my accent, my voice was called sexy,
and I couldn't help but think of my mother,
still repeating words for emphasis,
as if the more she speaks, the faster
she will gain approval;
while I've become
an exotic dish,
expected to fill
him.

I used to want to be more like my mother
Now she wants to be more like me.

II

The females in my family are plagued
with unsatisfactory lives,
doomed by inaction
and regret.
Sometimes I think of the sacrifices
my tribal ancestors have made,
both physically and ritually;
always throwing out
tongues,
words,
hearts,
bodies.
Haven't we already given too much?

III

The kitchen is where one learns womanhood.
My Papa says I should know my place.
He said, that way,
I will find a man.
But what about my chosen place?
Like with her,
her sheets,
her bed.
Our sheets,
our bed.
I learned womanhood the day
I learned her.

IV

I am an angry woman
because I love my culture,
but hate its
bind,
its grip,
its harshness,
its unforgiving reverence to religion,
its force.
Because I have been taught to be quiet.
Because there is nothing beautiful about silence.
Because I no longer want to be like my mother;
docile,
quiet,
graceful.
Her throat,
full of everything she's ever had to swallow,
because that's what good women do.

V

I am still learning how to be a woman.

VI
There are days I don't want to be a woman.

VII

My mother pleads with me to find my spirituality.
She says that is all I will inherit
but I often question the value of her God;
question if her prayers hold any worth
when she still goes to sleep wondering
when father will tell her he loves her
for the first time after twenty-three years,
when she will stop feeling used on nights when
all she craves is a conversation,
when she will begin to feel like a woman
and not another piece of unfinished furniture.

How many times must you share your body,
before you begin to feel the confirmation
of your own existence?

VIII

My sister wants to die.
She is only 13.
She doesn't feel smart enough,
Pretty enough,
Loved enough.
She doesn't feel *enough*.
She thinks she takes up too much space.

I'm beginning to sense a pattern.

IX

I stopped wanting to be like my mother,
like my aunt,
like my grandmother,
and I started wanting to be more like me.

X
Some days, I still wonder
If I am woman enough.

As young women, we are never taught how to love our bodies, only how to protect them. Equivocally, we begin to demand invisibility, believe submission and silence are key to survival; and that is when we begin to suffer.

-our bodies are not the enemy

La Rosa

Brown girl,
don't let them tell you
that there is wrongness in your magic.

Your beauty also cradles
thorns,
blood,
pain,
and the struggle of every brown girl
before you.

Don't they know,
that is what makes a brown girl?

El Hombre Llego

They say women in my culture are stronger,
because our marriages last longer.
We are grounded roots,
perennial spirits you cannot unearth.

But I met the only man I thought I could love,
before I knew wrapping roots around bodies
was no different
than wilting.

His light,
I was told,
would nourish.
It would be how you sprout into womanhood,
how you matured and ripened,
how you bloomed and grew,
how you made your parents proud,
how you found happiness,
like the women
who married sharpened scythes.

But see what happens
when we are stolen from the soil;
our petals plucked,
our hearts dissected,
when we are no longer raw and pure, vivacious.

See what happens
when they've picked their bounty,
filled their stomachs with our nectar,
discarded our moribund remains.

When you find us in *mercados olvidados*,
do not ask us why we wither.

I am not what has happened to me.
I am not responsible for you leaving,
for my father refusing to stay.
I cannot teach my mother happiness.
I am not to blame for the lingering night.
I am not the taunting sea,
holding hostage our secrets.
I am not my failures, my past.
I am not the broken pieces.
I am still learning how to believe
in my own wholeness.

-reparations

The value of my fruit should not be measured by its ability to delight your feeble tongue.

-exotic

They like the *idea* of you,

    if only you could take a little less,

        be a little more

-shapeshifter

Brujería

I take my chances,
accept whatever it was
that was cast upon me,
wear it with poise and grace.
My family is convinced,
that on the day I stopped breathing,
and the black rooster
disappeared in front
of our truck,
it was a omen
for all bad things that were to come.

Brujería
explained the sudden
inclination for all things
sinful-
my ungodly desires,
my throbbing hunger for flesh
not seasoned for me.
On that same day
a priest's prayers are believed to have
restored me,
brought back the color to my
reptilian skin,
settled my coldness.

They tried to bury me with guilt
and shame
but fearless women are already born
with the ability
to orchestrate a fake death,
to live unscathed.

I can teach you a thing or two
about pain and suffering,
about misterios y milagros,
about bypassing divine intervention to survive.

I can teach you about god and demons,
about how I create and exorcise them both
within myself.

Think of me this way;
I am a spell you cannot banish.

What happens to my body seems to be dictated by the state and what it thinks is best for me. My actions, for as long as I can remember, have been controlled by tradition and culture. My belief system has been set up by others and manipulated by the expectation of religion. But my mind is my own and I find comfort in knowing it remains untouched.

-only in my mind am I safe

I cannot begin to tell you
how many lines I have drawn
across words about ~~belonging~~.

My soul exists with los dioses
My body is waiting to be

        fouhd.

For my father, still learning how to spell my n a m e

-growth

Slaughter

What is the difference between
swine in slaughterhouses and men
without homelands?
Both waiting
to be rescued.

I have seen the blood of both swine and man,
tired hands,
slumped masses.
My mother says their eyes are too close to human,
which is why she could no longer send volts
into their temples.

My father knows his way with knives.
Sunday mornings spent
sharpening the kitchen knives proudly.
Twenty-two years of time spent perfecting his craft.
Twenty-two years bathed in blood.

His calloused hands speak a lifetime of conversation,
saying things like,
"become somebody;
don't end up like me,
spilling blood on cutting tables,"
like,
"this is not the American Dream,"
like,
"I cannot afford to retire."

I wonder if my mother ever thought of their blood
when birthing six children-
she told me stories of carving life
from the wombs of deceased mothers.

Carcasses of profit.

Boiled buckets of shortened lives.
Those bloodied hands still knew how to
hold a child tenderly, over and over again.
Instinctually, as if she knew how fragile our lives
would, too, become in America.

It is no secret,
this country enjoys the spilling of blood;
never interested in its difference between
the black man, brown man, and swine.
It always looks the same: mostly useless,
except when used to prove
the breaking of a species and kind.
That is what success looks like.

Soon, the knives will retire.
And my father's story will always be about
blood, death, and working hands.

And yet, I wish I knew why I still do not know how to
answer the question, "what do your parents do?"

A day spent shadowing,
the smell of death vividly haunting my dreams.
Rows of white costumes, a compelling juxtaposition
too perfect, it would almost seem made up.
It was before then, I was scared of the blood,
but now I know why I have spent a lifetime
trying to discard these putrid memories.

My mother and father have seen blood
for too long.

Decades spent in bloodied rooms,
bloodied walls, and shoes, and bodies.
Paused embraces for cleansing.
Yet crimson in their ears;
some marks of war will never see peace.

I dream of blood,
oceans of it,
wondering when my parents will stop bleeding,
stop drowning, wake up and feel alive.

Is America to blame for the carnage
or was this always the only life
they were destined to live
each time they open their mouths?

Are their tongues too other,
hair too *dark*,
too *thick*,
their skin too *suspect?*

If there is no difference between
swine in slaughterhouses
and men without homelands, tell me-
are my prayers for their escape in vain?

I am still waiting for
apologies I will never recieve,
words that will never be spoken.
I am waiting to forgive,
I am waiting for my time to heal.

-spring will come

I have tasted autonomy,
and I know
I will never go hungry again.

In my chest, a storm is
brewing, but you will only
see the sun.

The rabid dog will soon be gone.

For the days I confuse your blessings for curses, and my worries blind me of your gifts.

-an apology to the universe

Let us not be defined by recycled compliments,
or the lack of them, but by what we
ultimately choose to become.

-sisterhood

Portate bien. Un día vamos a ir al pueblo todos. Alla se vive mejor. Te pareces a tu abuela. Peinate bien. Todavía no sabes cocinar? Por cuánto tiempo vas a quedarte en donde estas? Comete todo, poquito a poquito. Para que vas al colegio, si es un robo? No te olvides de tu papa. Que te quiere. Que Dios te bendiga.

Otra Vez Con Mis Poemas de Cultura
(Here I Go Again with My Culture Poems)

This is another culture poem
about arroz con leche, piñatas, tacos, y wetbacks.
About how my bronze brown skin is not the right skin.
About how my tongue is not the right tongue.
About bleaching
the tongue,
the hair,
like the white of my eyes.
Like goodness,
like proper,
like permitted.
Like unquestioned,
like rights,
like power,
like privilege.
Like the solution to police brutality
found inside a can of Pepsi.
About how words don't translate
out for my Ma to understand;
the joke is not funny en Español.
This is another culture poem about
accents, and fiestas, and how my
pa's botas were once embarrassing in public.
About how I still cry when I remember
how I used to be ashamed
when kids called me a beaner.
Now I wear that title como una luchadora
and her first champion belt.
This is another culture poem
about how fitting in with the white kids
is nothing close to fitting in.

About how going to la escuela
does not mean turning your back
on your raíces.
About how nobody seems to understand that.
A poem about how bettering yourself
doesn't make you any less brown.
About how you don't want to not be brown.
This is a culture poem about being tired
of things like nopales, sombreros, y Frida Kahlo
being commercialized
by gluttonous corporations.
This is a culture poem
about my heritage adorning frat parties,
about it being used as an excuse
for drink specials on a holiday
we don't even celebrate.
This is another culture poem
about borders,
about familias separadas,
about meeting my grandfather only once,
about forgetting my grandfather.
This is another culture poem about
the American dream turned
nightmare
when I learned to
rip myself apart
to feel whole.
About the word "deportation"
tasting sour
in the mouths
of those who are
only trying to
Survive.
This is another culture poem,
and it is not my last.

what sadness, to exist in two places and not know what it is to belong

The Other Mexico

Shakes me up,
bullies coins of ethnic from my pockets;
convinces me to love pizza,
forget tortillas,
says fajitas the wrong way.

Changes my name,
smooths my r's,
tells me to sit straight
be quiet,
accept,
accept,
accept.

The other Mexico,
teaches me to lie,
forget my words,
defines beauty.

Steals my food,
my art,
steals my skin;
wears it to the gala,
to the beach,
to the photoshoot,
calls it her own.

And when she is home,
she sheds it off,
hangs it up,
and goes to sleep
in safety.

You scream borders while you erase
My ancestors' demand
To stop taking what is not
Yours.
Have you forgotten America, too, was ours?

-conquest is still considered war

How many miles until I feel at home?

A Family Portrait

I like to imagine an alternative history,
one where my ancestors fall in love.
Hand in hand, they dance down antiquated streets
that one day I would visit,
indigenous and new-worldly woven together by time.
The men, on a quest to conquer hearts, not bodies,
and the women, wild currents.

But the years of blood are evident.
Our last names,
violaceous bruises,
residual scars.

Our children
still do not speak of peace.

-all is fair in love and war

Weathered

You ask if I know where I come from. I remember the death of my father's dreams, the sand, the sun -- how it gives and takes -- I remember the river of both water and blood. I remember.   How could I forget?

How could I forget the women in sus casitas, folding laundry, talking to their neighbors about no se que, secretly longing for their husbands, whose faces they swear they will not erase. Years consumed with tired prayers, their homes, makeshift altars, hungry for the ring of the phone.

How could I forget -- my grandmother who I only met in photographs, her eyes a sadness you cannot mistake. The day she passed on, alone, I bet she thought of her children, the years of longing, them too busy with their lives on the other side. They say she died of a collapsed lung, and I wonder if she spent her days holding her breath-- waiting.

My Ma also had dreams, dreams she still brings up at the dinner table, spoken with her mouth full, careful not to be understood. I know she never guessed her life would be consumed with mops and rags, whitening up spaces where she is not welcome.

I cannot forget the fear of those too criminal for dreaming, too desperate to give up. Every time I think of them, I imagine that if their exile had a sound, it would be of sobbing mothers and fathers -- guilt wrapped around their conquered throats.

I know where I come from -- a place that only knows of my existence when I call for it on nights when I feel the shedding of my skin, the swelling of my tongue evicting words, both becoming foreign. The place whispers reminders of my roots. It tells me it is still waiting for me to come home.

I am beginning to feel more universe, less human.

-todo revoluciona

What side do you stand on,
when your whole is *not* whole,
when your parts have only known war?

-Nepantla

del otro lado

In my notes,
I write the recipe to my ma's enchiladas
next to thoughts about my shithole country.
I talk about how I think in Spanish
but dream in English,
and for that I feel guilty.
I've been hiding the photograph
of Our Lady of Guadalupe,
my ma gave me for Christmas,
in the closet
because it does not match
our mid-century modern decor.
My ma told me she would bless
my new American home.
But I still pray to her
in silence.
Ask her for forgiveness.
Tell her, maybe one day,
we will both be free.

Odes to My Tongue

Pink twister,
who wrestles the language
of my ancestors-
tough as a cactus,
sweet as its prickly pear

You dare to crave the taste of freedom,
even when you are threatened
into submission.

I owe you
my wisdom
and my struggle,
for had I not learned to wake your
Zapatista song.
I would not be heard
from mountains.

The giver of voice,
and of the words you only
learn from angry Latina mothers,
whose bellies swarm with
orphaned maldiciones,
waiting to be rescued.

Well of opportunity,
your versatility,
a translated ability
for increased worth
in markets
I have yet to flaunt my fruits in.

Treasure box
of memory,
ancient scripts
of ancestry,
unraveling with
each movement
of your instinctual
dance.

My stubborn hero,
your persistence,
an itchy reminder
to never forget
you,
your battles,
your gifts.

They call it politics to distract you from engaging in it.
Inferring that a certain kind of knowledge is needed to
understand. But to know, instinctually that a person is not
culpable for doing whatever is within their means to survive
is simple sympathy and human nature. This is not something that
is taught, but hate is. Do not let divisive words meant to make
you feel inferior, make you second guess your instinctual call-
ing to care. Do not let them blind you from the truth.

This border wall is a war tactic, here to protect what is a
land that was taken from the hands of those who honored it.
It is a ridiculous notion to give ownership to a land meant for
all. Greed is warfare. Let us look into the window of the past.

Remember why walls have been built. Why blood has been
shed. Why foundations of fear have been built. Do not
confuse manipulation for civic duty. it is not your civic
duty to deny life to those who have risked it since their
birth. (at the hands of wild dogs, hungry for power)

There are borders, physical and INVISIBLE, but LOVE does
not have to be.

I am sick of being haunted by the faces of pain

This Is What Thirst Looks Like

a man tucked away in the hollow belly of a semi-truck, his sweaty hands gripping his father's funeral rosary. He closes his eyes and thinks of opportunity, as he listens to women and children exhale as they are swallowed into oblivion. One by one, they become mere bodies who once had names only the ones back home will remember.

a boy's body floats down the river, swollen with time. Collateral for unpaid debts, for his father thinking survival could be free.

a woman travels fifteen-hundred miles on foot to meet with eagerness, a future only possible upon crossing, instead she is welcomed by the barrel of a gun.
This is the last thing she will ever see.

a young girl's wish of lighter skin and freedom paints pictures of promises in her dreams. She is now in the hands of men much older. Her fragmented body, devoured at night only to be regurgitated by morning, expected to feel whole. She often wonders how a dream can turn into a nightmare.

your distant home on fire, and America, a watering hole you can only witness, like a mirage of salvation, already on reserve.

Things We Don't Talk About

Mi Papa
wears cowboy boots,
the kind that make him look
hombre.
I don't blame him.
He has to feel dominant,
since his tongue is not.
His hands,
the epitome of labor,
yet he still cannot
hold his pen the "right way,"
he still practices his loops.

ONE DAY A NEW DAWN
WILL COME AND
I WILL
MEET MY PEOPLE
FACE TO FACE AND WE
WILL BOTH KNOW HOME
AND WE WILL NOT
WORRY ABOUT CROSSING
OVER TO THE OTHER SIDE.

Tonight is one of those nights, where I dream of war and taste the blood.

I wanted to write a love poem about loss,
about a heart that gave until it ran empty, about lovers
that dropped like baby teeth; one after the other.
But what is more tragic than being gifted a body
you can't recognize? It, an island
home without a mailbox, a landline sliced in two.
What is more tragic
than never having feared being swallowed whole
by the sea, and its gluttonous belly of pain?

-Babel, the Body I Do Not Understand

Mujer Magia

I am a son as soon as my father learns of my existence. He is too afraid to raise a daughter. He is still afraid to love his daughter. So I set myself on fire.

When I cut my hair in rebellion, each strand a standard I no longer strive for, he travels through his memory, trying to recall the sins that gave him me. He says I am a fool-- men cannot love women like me,
who are not afraid to burn.

In our culture, men cannot swallow whole the concept of love. They do not give - they only take. They only know of colonizing - land, water, *bodies*. I do not become woman when I share, surrender, my goods to them - I am not woman the day they are stolen.

I am not only woman the day the blood comes. but when it does. I do not scream. Do not cry. I invite it in. See how I create a war. See how I survive it.

How do I teach a man to love me
when he doesn't love himself?
When I finally have a brother, I make sure to tell him I love him until he says it back.

When I have a sister, I look to make sure she does not have my mother's eyes,
maybe then my father will look at her.

The other women in my life compare their flames to mine. They say I am one of the lucky ones. but men still hunt me. I find traces of them everywhere. Sometimes even in myself.

When I finally outlive war-
when I no longer feel the burning --

I will come to realize that I am woman by nature, that I am gifted an incomparable blessing. I am power, I am voice, sustenance, beauty and joy, I am human, I am alive, I am the universe.

I do not believe I am woman on someone else's accord, I do not let them take credit for my magic.

The day will come when man will envy the ashes – meanwhile I will be busy becoming the ocean, as a fierce reminder of what happens when they think I can be tamed.

My Childhood Home

Your white walls,
and crooked sidewalks.
Wobbly dancefloors
for fiestas
with birthday cakes
I once spilled tears into,
wished for things I can no longer remember.

And the weekends spent
watching el Rebaño Sagrado
on the television
my ma brought with her from California.
She says it was the first thing she owned
in America.
How can I forget the re-runs of novelas
on Univision,
with star women
we aspired to be.
Imitating characters, playing house,
waiting for the husband
who has made a home
with another.

This was what we knew of love.

Yet you witnessed it;
me in all my bruised teenage glory,
my fingers reaching for long lost lovers
in the dark chambers of your heart.

My body gently shaking off each loss,
wiping blood from my skinned knees.
Wanting badly
to be seen,
to be loved.
To be anything but
careful,
patient,
predictable.

How I miss the nights when the starless skies
hugged us,
and danced with us our favorite rancheras,
when we were not yet burdened
by the incessant pain of growing up.

I like to think we have forgotten
that you, small-town Nebraska home,
made us easy targets
for confederate flag bigotry,
etching nightmares of hatred in
the walls of our memory.

I want to go back,
to the years
I pretended to be asleep until I heard my name
in my father's prayers,
when I still believed that he could save me.
I hope these things linger;
the smell of tortillas y cafecito,
my ma's cucurrucucú,
mariachi tongue,
our morning call
and scattered burial sites for our pet fish--
stick crosses swallowed deep by your soil
--behind la yerba buena.
Before we knew nothing stayed,
before we knew not everything
can be buried.

Tengo la luna y las estrellas,
Y la luz de ellas me guían hacia ti.

-se que no estoy sola

To All My Sisters of Color

I dreamt of you, with your hair so free,
reaching for the sky.
Your skin finally breathing without permission.
You smiled at yourself in the mirror,
said something about how you'd like to
love yourself
and you believed it.

El Valiente

Every time my pa would drive
with me in the backseat,
he would be silent,
except for the brief moments
of broken prayers.
I often wondered if he imagined
himself on a dirt road
somewhere in Miraplanes, Mexico;
searching for lost cattle,
or sheep,
or for himself.

His bracero hands,
tainted with earth
that he'd be proud of.

My interruptions would come
in the form of questions
when I caught him
whispering to himself
he wanted to go back.

"Are you proud of us?"

It is painful
watching a root grow
where it is not wanted.

I keep going back to the day
in my abuelo's old pickup
on our way home from a charreada.
My pa's rodeo jeans and sombrero
matching my brother's,
and I sitting quietly in the backseat,
with muddy boots.
My pa saying,
"this is the last time you will get boots,"
a prophecy interpreted,
"girls aren't meant for things like this."

Now,
when I dream,
I see revolution in his eyes,
Zapata-esque visions.
I see him
escaping *pal otro lado,*
full of color
like an upgraded tv,
no static.

And I wake up and wonder
is that what a valiente looks like?
A man
with a lasso and some hope.

THERE ARE GHOSTS WITHIN THESE PAGES.

Angelica Mercado is an artist and poet currently residing in Sioux Falls, SD. She is a Mexican-born, American-raised "nepantlera" who writes and creates art about the experience of the "in-between." Her work has been published in the Briar Cliff Review, Cream City Review, Acentos Review, Roanoke Review, Glass Poetry Press, among others.

"Living in the Midwest, in a traditional Catholic Mexican household, has brought with it many hurdles. My work not only highlights what it's like to be a queer woman in a situation like this, but a woman in general. At times, machismo and traditional expectations become too difficult to ignore when they stem from a culture that has gone too long supporting these ideals. How do you survive it? You write about it. You educate the public about the issues, and you empower others to rise up and fight a flawed and damaging system of oppression that not only affects women culturally, but socially. As a Latina woman in the United States, you have two options, to either live in the shadows, or learn to stand up for yourself as a woman, a Latina, and as a human being, all while absorbing and celebrating the beautiful parts of your authentic self."

I want to thank everyone and everything that inspired the beginning, middle, and end of this book.

The faculty at Briar Cliff University, specifically Ryan Allen. My family and friends near and far, Olivia Ford, Chip & Jennifer Carlson, Nathan Hittle, Melanie Mergen, Janet Pischke, Sasha McDowell, Robert Swaney, and Harsan Publishing.

Acknowledgements

My gratitude goes to the editors of the following journals, in which poems in this book, sometimes in earlier versions, first appeared:

Briar Cliff Review: "Tongues" and "El Valiente"

Roanoke Review: "On Being Woman (in ten parts)"

Glass Poetry Press - Poets Resist Series: "Freedom Is a Fleeting Thing"

Z Publishing House: "Mujer Magia"

CPSIA information can be obtained
at www.ICGtesting.com
Printed in the USA
FSHW020303290319